I0838045

Ready for Anything: A Comprehensive
Guide to Managing Domestic Emergencies

Foreword:

Why Prepare for Everything?
Preparing for everything is essential in a world
where climate change and climate engineering are
becoming ever-present realities.
With the artificial control of weather and the
use of technologies to manipulate the climate,
such as geoengineering and other advanced
techniques, the natural balance of the
environment is being altered, creating new and
unpredictable conditions.

These interventions, often designed to mitigate
global warming or manage extreme weather events,
can nevertheless have unforeseen side effects.
For example, climate manipulation could cause
storms, floods, droughts, or anomalous
meteorological phenomena in areas where they were
once rare or absent.
Having a well-structured home emergency plan
becomes a necessity because adverse events are no
longer entirely natural and, therefore, may
strike with less warning.

Being prepared means not only facing events we
are familiar with, such as blackouts or fires,
but also adapting to new emergencies that may be
triggered by artificial climate interventions.

Faced with a future where climate unpredictability may increase, prevention becomes the first and most important form of protection. We cannot control everything, but we can control our level of preparedness.

Happy reading,
Simone Azzurri

Chapter 1: Introduction to Domestic Emergencies
Definition of domestic emergency
Why being prepared is important
Common examples of domestic emergencies (blackouts, floods, fires, plumbing failures)

Chapter 2: Creating a Family Emergency Plan
Communication and responsibility among family members
Establishing meeting points in case of evacuation
Simulations and emergency drills

Chapter 3: Emergency Kit: What It Should Contain
Essential items for an emergency kit (flashlights, batteries, water, non-perishable food, medicine)
Where to store the kit and how to regularly update it
Useful tools for different types of emergencies

Chapter 4: Electrical Blackouts: How to Handle Them

What to do immediately during a blackout

How to protect electronic devices and appliances

Alternative solutions for lighting and heating

Chapter 5: Floods and Water Leaks

How to prevent flooding in your home

What to do in case of flooding

How to manage water damage

Chapter 6: Domestic Fires: Prevention and Quick Response

Preventing electrical and gas fires

Proper use of fire extinguishers and smoke alarms

Evacuation plan in case of fire

Chapter 7: Plumbing Failures: How to Handle Them

What to do in case of pipe bursts or leaks

Emergency tools for plumbing failures

When to call a professional

Chapter 8: Protection from Intruders: Home Security

Security systems and alarms

How to secure doors and windows

Personal safety measures during an intrusion

Chapter 9: Environmental Risks: Storms, Earthquakes, and Other Natural Disasters

Preparing for storms and extreme weather events
How to respond during an earthquake
What to do after a natural disaster

Chapter 10: Managing Psychological Emergencies

How to stay calm during an emergency
Stress management techniques in panic situations
How to support your family during a crisis

Continuing with the basics, starting with
Chapter 1: Introduction to Domestic Emergencies

Introduction to Domestic Emergencies.
Domestic emergencies are unexpected events that can jeopardize the safety of your home and the people living in it.

These situations require a rapid response and can include electrical failures, water leaks, fires, earthquakes, or intrusions.

While some of these events may seem rare, others can occur more frequently than one might think, making it essential to be prepared.

Many people tend to underestimate the likelihood of a domestic emergency until they experience one.

Without adequate preparation, even a situation
that could easily be managed can turn into a
disaster, causing financial damage or putting
people's safety at risk.
The goal of this book is to help you understand
potential risks and prepare effectively so that
you always know what to do in the face of an
emergency.

Being prepared means having a clear plan and the
right tools to react promptly and minimize
damage.

Knowing how to behave in an emergency not only
allows you to save valuable time but also reduces
the stress and confusion that often accompany
these situations.

Additionally, preparation offers a great
psychological advantage: knowing that everything
is under control allows you to face difficulties
with greater calm.

However, preparation is not just about responding
quickly.
Many domestic emergencies can be prevented
through simple actions and practical measures.

For example, regularly checking electrical and plumbing systems, installing smoke detectors, and stocking up on essential materials in case of emergency are key steps to prevent small problems from turning into big disasters.

Domestic emergencies can present themselves in many forms.
An electrical blackout, for example, can leave you without lighting and access to appliances for hours or even days.
Without a plan, managing a blackout can be complicated, especially in the case of prolonged power outages.

Another common emergency is water leaks, which can result from a broken pipe or a flaw in the plumbing system.
If not addressed promptly, these leaks can cause structural damage to the house.

Domestic fires also pose a real threat and can be triggered by electrical malfunctions, gas leaks, or kitchen mishaps.

Having fire extinguishers on hand, knowing how to use them correctly, and having a clear evacuation plan can make the difference between a tragedy and an incident managed successfully.

Being ready to face emergencies doesn't mean
expecting the worst, but having the confidence
that you can protect what is most important to
you, reducing the impact that unexpected events
might have on your life.

Chapter 2: Creating a Family Emergency Plan
Having a well-defined family emergency plan is
essential for handling any unexpected situation
in a coordinated and safe manner.
Domestic emergencies can occur at any time, and
when they do, time is of the essence.
Knowing exactly what to do, where to go, and how
to communicate with loved ones can make the
difference between orderly management of the
situation and total chaos.

The first step in creating an effective plan is involving the entire family. Everyone should be aware of their role in case of an emergency and know what actions to take.

This process should include the division of responsibilities: who is in charge of calling emergency services, who ensures that everyone is safe, and who handles turning off any systems to prevent further damage.

Each person should have a specific task to avoid confusion during critical moments.

Communication is one of the most important aspects of the plan. In an emergency, the family might be in different areas of the house or even outside.

Establishing a secure method to stay in touch is essential.
One option is to designate a safe and easily accessible meeting point for everyone.

This could be the garden, an area near the house, or even a particularly safe room inside.

The important thing is that every family member knows where to go in case of an emergency.

In addition to meeting points, having an evacuation plan is crucial.

Knowing the safest escape routes in case of fire, earthquake, or other emergencies can save lives.

Every room should have a planned exit, which could include doors, windows, or other emergency exits.

It is critical to ensure that every family member knows how to use these exits safely.

Finally, an often-overlooked part of the emergency plan is simulation.

It's not enough to have a written plan; it must be practiced regularly to ensure everyone is comfortable with their tasks and knows how to move in the event of a real emergency.

Organizing regular drills helps verify that the plan works and allows for any necessary adjustments based on new needs or changes in the home.

A family emergency plan not only ensures that everyone knows what to do in a crisis but also strengthens the sense of security.

Knowing there's a clear strategy can reduce the stress and anxiety that often accompany emergencies, allowing the entire family to face the unexpected with greater calm and clarity.

Chapter 3: Preparing a Complete Emergency Kit

When it comes to household emergencies, one of the most crucial aspects is having a well-stocked emergency kit that is always within reach.

An emergency kit is not just a collection of useful items; it's a true lifeline that can make the difference between a dangerous situation and one resolved safely.

Preparing a complete kit requires planning and care, as it needs to include everything that you and your family might need to face a wide range of emergencies.

An emergency kit should be designed to cover basic needs for at least 72 hours, which is generally the time required for rescue or recovery services to intervene during crisis situations.

This kit should be easily accessible and placed in a location known to all family members, preferably near an emergency exit or in a part of the house that remains safe during disasters such as earthquakes, fires, or floods.

The first thing to consider when preparing an emergency kit is water.

Water is essential for survival, and in case of an emergency, you might find yourself without

access to safe water sources.
It is important to have enough drinking water for
at least three days, estimating about one gallon
(four liters) per person per day.

This should cover both drinking and personal
hygiene needs.
Additionally, it's useful to have water
purification systems, such as tablets or portable
filters, in case you need to rely on unsafe water
sources.

Another crucial element is food.
Non-perishable foods are essential in an
emergency kit.

Choose long-lasting foods that don't require
cooking or refrigeration, such as energy bars,
dried fruits, canned vegetables and beans, or
canned foods.

Make sure to have a manual can opener in the kit
in case of a power outage.

It's also important to consider the dietary needs
of all family members, such as allergies or food
intolerances, to ensure everyone has access to
safe food.

In addition to basic needs like food and water,
the kit should include useful tools to handle any
situation.

A flashlight with spare batteries is essential, as many emergencies involve power outages.

Having a battery-powered or hand-crank radio will keep you informed of official communications regarding the emergency and evacuation instructions.

It's also essential to have tools such as a multi-purpose knife, a wrench for turning off gas or water systems, and duct tape for temporary repairs.

The medical aspect should not be overlooked. A well-stocked first aid kit is essential for treating wounds, cuts, or bruises that may occur during an emergency.

The kit should include bandages, sterile gauze, adhesive bandages, disinfectants, scissors, latex gloves, an emergency blanket, and medications for treating common emergencies such as pain relievers or antihistamines.

If anyone in the family has specific medical needs, such as prescription medications taken regularly, make sure to include them in the kit, along with a supply sufficient for at least three days.

Basic hygiene supplies should also be included in

the emergency kit.

Wet wipes, toilet paper, plastic bags, and personal hygiene products such as soap or hand sanitizers are useful for maintaining proper cleanliness during an extended emergency.

This not only helps to preserve health but also morale, especially in highly stressful situations.

An often overlooked aspect is the need for important documents.
In an emergency, you might need to evacuate your home quickly, leaving behind everything that is not strictly necessary.

However, documents such as ID cards, insurance policies, bank documents, or property certificates are crucial for your and your family's security.

Preparing a copy of these documents, both in paper and digital format, and storing them in a waterproof pouch or on a USB drive could be vital in case of loss of access to your home or during evacuation.

Besides material goods, the emergency kit should include items for psychological comfort, especially if you have children.

Games, books, coloring books, or other small
entertainment items can help reduce anxiety and
stress during a prolonged emergency.

For adults, having a small supply of cash can be
useful in case banking services or electronic
payments are unavailable.

Keeping the kit updated is another important
aspect of preparation.

Food, water, and some medications have expiration
dates and must be replaced regularly.

Additionally, changes in family needs might
require updating the kit, such as the arrival of
a new family member or changes in someone's
health condition.

It's a good idea to check the kit at least once a
year, verify that everything is in order, and
replace anything expired or worn out.

In conclusion, a well-organized and updated
emergency kit is a key component to facing any
crisis with peace of mind.

Knowing that you have everything necessary to
protect your family and manage the first 72 hours
of an emergency gives you confidence and
tranquility, allowing you to act with clarity and

determination.

Preparing the kit is a small effort that can make
a big difference when needed most.

Chapter 4: Safe Evacuation Strategies

In an emergency, knowing how and when to evacuate
can save lives.

One of the first things to consider when
preparing for any type of emergency is planning a
safe evacuation strategy.

When faced with events like fires, floods,
earthquakes, or other situations that put home
safety at risk, having an evacuation plan ready
and known by all family members is essential.

In this chapter, we will explore the key steps to
plan a smooth and safe escape, ensuring everyone
knows how to act in a crisis.

The first thing to do is identify the safest exit
routes from your home.

Each room should have at least two evacuation
paths, if possible.

Typically, these include the main or secondary
door, but in extreme situations, windows or
emergency exits may be necessary.

If your house has multiple floors, also consider
using emergency ladders to safely descend from
upstairs windows.

It is important that every family member,
including children, knows where these exits are
and how to use them quickly and safely.

Once the escape routes are identified, it is essential to establish external meeting points where all family members can gather after evacuation.

This helps quickly verify if someone has been left behind or needs assistance. The meeting point should be safe, easily accessible, and at a sufficient distance from the house to avoid dangers such as fires, collapses, or other imminent threats.

It could be a garden, a neighbor's yard, or a nearby square. Ensure that everyone knows where this location is and that they can reach it even in low visibility or under stress.

During evacuation, staying calm is crucial.

Even if the situation seems dire, panic can lead to wrong and dangerous decisions.

Planning ahead and having regular drills helps create an automatic response, reducing stress when a real emergency occurs.

Participating in evacuation drills with the family allows everyone to become familiar with the plan and makes the entire process more natural.

Simulating different scenarios, such as evacuations in the dark or during a mock gas emergency, will better prepare you to handle any complications.

An often-overlooked aspect of evacuation is paying attention to the most vulnerable, such as young children, the elderly, or people with disabilities.

If there are people in your family who might have difficulty moving quickly, it's essential to plan in advance how to assist them.

It might be useful to designate a family member or neighbor specifically to help these individuals during evacuation.

Also, if you have pets, including them in the plan is equally important.

Ensure you have a safe way to transport them, such as crates or carriers, to prevent them from getting lost or injured during the evacuation.

External conditions can greatly affect the
evacuation strategy.

For example, in the case of a fire, it may not
always be safe to use stairs or go through
certain areas of the house due to smoke or
flames.

In such cases, it might be necessary to adopt a
passive defense position until help arrives, such
as sealing yourself in a room and sealing door
gaps to prevent smoke from entering.

Weather conditions, such as heavy rain or strong
winds, can also pose an obstacle, so it's
important to consider various scenarios and adapt
the strategy accordingly.

Another key factor is the speed at which you can leave the house.

In some situations, like fires or collapses, every second counts. It is crucial to avoid wasting time trying to retrieve valuables or personal belongings.

The safety of the family must be the top priority.

In this regard, it's advisable to keep emergency bags ready near the escape routes.

These bags should contain the essentials for surviving in the immediate days following the evacuation, such as water, food, a flashlight, a change of clothes, and copies of important documents.

Having a bag ready allows you to act quickly without having to think about what to bring.

After evacuation, the danger is not always over.

You may have to wait hours or days before being able to return home, so it's important to be prepared for what happens after leaving.

In cases of natural disasters like earthquakes or floods, structures may not be safe for a long time, and you may need to seek temporary shelter at emergency centers or with friends and relatives. In these cases, communication is crucial.

Having a charged cell phone or portable charger in the emergency kit allows you to stay in touch with rescue teams and receive critical updates.

If the power or phone network is down, a battery-powered or hand-crank radio can be very helpful for receiving information from authorities.

Evacuation can be one of the most critical phases during an emergency, and every detail must be planned in advance to ensure everyone's safety.

The primary goal is always to get away from danger as quickly as possible, while maintaining an orderly and rational approach.

Planning, practice, and flexibility are the keys to managing even the most extreme situations without putting your life or that of your loved ones at risk.

Chapter 5: Essential Survival Kits

Being prepared for an emergency doesn't just mean
knowing how to react and where to go; it also
involves having the right resources at hand.

A well-organized survival kit is one of the
fundamental tools for facing any kind of crisis.

Whether it's a prolonged power outage, a natural
disaster, or a sudden emergency, having
everything you need to get through the first few
days is crucial for staying calm and safe.

In this chapter, we will see how to create a
complete and functional survival kit, analyzing
each item and explaining why it's essential.

The core of every survival kit is made up of basic supplies that cover primary needs: water, food, shelter, first aid, and communication tools.

One of the first things to consider is water supply. The human body can go days without food but cannot survive long without water.

For this reason, it's vital to include at least three liters of water per person per day for at least three days.

It's advisable to store sealed bottles of drinking water, but if space is limited, an alternative could be to include water purification tablets or a portable filter to make water drinkable in emergency situations.

Non-perishable food is also an essential component of the kit. Ideally, food should be easy to store, nutritious, and ready to use without the need for cooking.

Energy bars, nuts, jerky, and canned meals are good options.

Be sure to include a manual can opener in case the food is packed in cans.

The key is to choose foods with a long shelf life that require little or no preparation, so you can eat under difficult conditions without electricity or kitchen tools.

Another key element of the kit is shelter.

In a natural disaster like an earthquake or hurricane, your home may no longer be safe, and you may need to seek outdoor refuge.

For this reason, your kit should include lightweight tents or waterproof tarps that can be used to create a temporary shelter.

Emergency thermal blankets are equally important, as they provide insulation in extreme cold and can be lifesaving in cases of exposure to low temperatures.

If space allows, including a warm sleeping bag or fleece blanket can make a big difference.

First aid is another critical aspect of a survival kit.

During an emergency, injuries, burns, or other accidents are common, so having a well-stocked kit on hand is essential.

Your first-aid kit should include various sizes of band-aids, sterile gauze, elastic bandages, disinfectants, scissors, tweezers, and sterile gloves.

Also, add over-the-counter painkillers, allergy medication, and basic medicines like antibiotic creams.

If anyone in your family has special medical conditions, be sure to include their essential medications and prescriptions.

Additionally, it's a good idea to add a first-aid guide to handle common situations like cuts, bruises, or fractures safely.

Besides supplies for physical survival,
communication is equally vital.

During a crisis, phone networks may be down, and
staying informed becomes difficult.

A battery-powered or crank radio allows you to
listen to updates from local authorities about
the situation's development and evacuation or
return home instructions.

A cell phone with a portable charger is also
indispensable for staying in contact with
emergency services and family members.

If possible, include a fully charged power bank
in the kit to ensure a power source during
prolonged blackouts.

As for lighting, battery-powered flashlights, LED
lamps, or long-lasting candles are essential for
safely getting through the night.

Hand-crank or solar-powered flashlights can be a
good option since they don't require replacement
batteries.

Be sure to have a hatchet or multi-function
knife, tools that can be useful for cutting,
digging, or building shelters.

Another often-overlooked element is hygiene.

Even in emergency conditions, maintaining a minimum level of personal hygiene helps prevent diseases and infections.

The kit should include wet wipes, antibacterial soap, toilet paper, garbage bags, and hand sanitizer.

If possible, also include surgical masks and disposable gloves, especially in case of health emergencies or environmental contamination.

It's important to remember that a survival kit is not a "one-size-fits-all" solution.

It must be tailored to your family's specific needs and the type of emergency you might face.

For example, if you live in an earthquake-prone area, you may want to add tools for removing debris or protective gear for the face and eyes.

On the other hand, if you live in a flood-prone area, it might be useful to include life jackets or sandbags to prevent water from entering your home.

Lastly, remember to regularly check and update your kit.

Food and water have expiration dates, and even some medications or medical supplies can deteriorate over time.

Set reminders to check the kit's contents every six months and replace any expired or damaged items.

Being prepared also means keeping the kit in perfect condition, ready to be used at any time.

Your survival kit is an investment in your family's safety, and having it ready could make the difference between being protected and finding yourself in a vulnerable situation during an emergency.

Planning for every eventuality also means being ready to respond quickly and with the right resources at hand.

Planning ahead allows you to face situations that could otherwise be disastrous with calm and security.

Chapter 6: Managing Health Emergencies

In an emergency, health and safety become top
priorities.

However, during a disaster, access to healthcare
facilities may be limited or even interrupted,
and professional medical care might not be
immediately available.

Therefore, it is crucial to be prepared to handle
common and potentially dangerous health
situations.

In this chapter, we will explore how to manage
household health emergencies with the tools at
hand, what preparations are useful to make in
advance, and how to stay calm in critical
situations.

Having a fully equipped first-aid kit is the essential first step in being ready to handle a wide range of health emergencies.

A standard first-aid kit should include sterile gauze, elastic bandages, adhesive bandages, disinfectants, scissors, tweezers, sterile gloves, and other basic items to treat cuts, scrapes, burns, and minor wounds.

It is also advisable to include a selection of over-the-counter medications such as pain relievers, antihistamines for allergic reactions, and indigestion remedies.

While these basic tools are crucial, a proper emergency health kit should be tailored to the specific needs of each family.

One of the first things to consider is any
chronic medical conditions or specific health
needs of family members.

If someone takes regular medications, it is
important to have a sufficient supply of those
medicines, enough for at least one to two weeks,
to cope with potential supply disruptions.

This is especially important for conditions like
diabetes, hypertension, or asthma, which require
constant monitoring and specific medications.

Additionally, it is useful to include emergency
medical devices, such as spare inhalers, insulin
syringes, and glucose meters for blood sugar
control.

Health emergencies during a disaster can range from minor accidents to more serious situations like fractures, deep wounds, or anaphylactic shock.

Knowing how to respond promptly and correctly can make a difference.

One of the most important aspects is knowing basic first-aid procedures.

For example, knowing how to properly bandage a bleeding wound can prevent infection or hemorrhage and save lives.

Fractures require immobilizing the affected limb to prevent further damage, while burns should be treated immediately with cold water and covered with sterile gauze to reduce the risk of infection.

In the case of more serious medical emergencies, it may not be possible to reach a hospital or call emergency services immediately.

Therefore, it is useful to have access to resources and knowledge that can help you make quick, informed decisions.

Having a first-aid manual on hand is essential for those without medical experience, but it is equally important to attend first-aid training courses before an emergency occurs.

Many organizations offer practical courses on how to deal with situations like choking, cardiopulmonary resuscitation (CPR), and other life-saving techniques.

These skills can prove invaluable when emergency services are not immediately available.

During a natural disaster or prolonged emergency, one of the major concerns is the spread of infectious diseases.

Personal hygiene and cleanliness of living spaces are crucial to maintain, even in difficult conditions.

Therefore, it is important to have a supply of hygiene materials such as antibacterial soap, hand sanitizers, masks, and gloves.

Additionally, having a system for waste and sewage management is advisable to prevent contamination and the spread of disease, especially if sanitary services are disrupted.

Another often overlooked, but vital, aspect is psychological support during emergencies.

Crises do not only affect the body but also the mind. Stress and anxiety can significantly impact a person's ability to manage an emergency situation.

Being in isolation or facing the loss of loved ones or your home can cause emotional trauma.

For this reason, it is useful to include stress-reduction techniques in your emergency plan, such as meditation or deep breathing exercises.

Additionally, openly discussing emergencies with family members and children can help reduce fear and uncertainty.

In some situations, it may be necessary to evacuate your home immediately due to a fire, flood, or earthquake.

In these cases, it is advisable to have a "go-bag," a portable emergency kit containing basic survival items for at least 72 hours.

In addition to medications, the go-bag should include copies of important personal documents, such as IDs, passports, and medical certificates.

It is also useful to keep a list of emergency contacts, with phone numbers for friends, relatives, and health services, to facilitate communication in case of need.

In conclusion, preparing for health emergencies means not only having the necessary tools and resources available but also knowing how to use them correctly.

Prevention, planning, and training are key elements in dealing with any medical crisis.

Investing time and effort in learning first-aid techniques and creating a well-equipped emergency kit will allow you to protect yourself and your family even in the most difficult situations.

Having these resources at hand and knowing the basics of medical assistance can make the difference between a positive outcome and a tragic one in crisis situations.

Chapter 7: Managing Food Resources

In emergency situations, managing food resources is crucial to ensuring survival and maintaining physical health and strength.

During an unexpected event, such as a natural disaster or a prolonged service interruption, access to food may become limited or even impossible.

Therefore, it's essential to prepare in advance by stockpiling adequate food supplies and learning how to properly manage and store these resources for an extended period.

One of the main aspects of preparation involves selecting the right foods for storage.

Not all types of food are suitable for long-term storage, so it's important to choose non-perishable products that can last for months or even years without spoiling.

These include items like dried legumes, pasta, rice, flour, cereals, canned food, and freeze-dried products.

Canned foods such as vegetables, legumes, soups, and meat are particularly useful because they have a long shelf life and can be consumed without requiring special preparation.

Whole grains like rice, oats, and buckwheat are also great for the long term, as they provide energy and are easy to cook.

It is also advisable to store a selection of foods rich in protein and healthy fats, such as nuts, seeds, and peanut butter, which are excellent sources of energy and essential nutrients.

In an emergency, the body may require more calories than usual due to stress or physical activity, and these high-energy foods can help maintain strength.

Additionally, consuming healthy fats contributes to maintaining mental and physical well-being, two crucial elements during a crisis.

In addition to choosing the right foods, proper storage of supplies is essential to avoid waste and spoilage.

Dry and canned foods should be stored in cool, dry environments, away from direct sunlight.

Extreme temperatures and humidity can accelerate the decomposition process or damage packaging, reducing the shelf life of the food.

Using airtight containers can prevent exposure to air and moisture, keeping supplies fresh for longer periods.

Investing in quality plastic or glass containers can make a difference, as they protect food from mold, insects, and rodents.

A crucial part of managing food resources during an emergency is meal planning.

Without proper planning, you may consume more food than necessary in the first few days, leaving you without supplies for the long term.

It is helpful to divide food reserves into portions that can cover a certain number of meals for each family member, considering both nutritional and caloric needs.

Once the resources are divided, following a meal schedule can help ensure controlled and regular consumption of food.

During a prolonged emergency, it may be necessary to prepare meals with limited equipment or without access to gas, electricity, or running water.

For this reason, it is important to have an alternative cooking source, such as a portable gas stove, a barbecue, or a wood stove. These tools allow you to cook even in the event of a power outage.

Make sure you always have a supply of fuel for these appliances, whether it's gas, wood, or charcoal.

Additionally, having durable pots and pans, ideal for cooking over an open flame or other unconventional heat sources, can be useful.

If food resources start to run low, it's important to have alternatives.

Having a home garden or small plot can be extremely useful for growing fresh vegetables and fruit independently.

Growing plants like tomatoes, zucchini, herbs, or potatoes requires relatively little space, and with the right care, can provide a supplemental food source over time.

Even in small spaces like balconies or terraces, you can create mini gardens using pots or raised containers.

Having a reserve of quality seeds and soil allows you to quickly start a garden, even in emergency situations.

If water availability becomes an issue, water conservation and management are essential to ensure that food can be cooked safely.

Having potable water and containers to collect it can prevent the use of contaminated water, which could lead to illness.

When water is scarce, it's helpful to prepare meals that require little or no water to cook, such as ready-to-eat canned foods.

It's always important to maintain an adequate water supply, calculating at least 2-3 liters per day per person, not only for drinking but also for cooking and personal hygiene.

Finally, in an emergency situation, the mental element plays an important role in managing food resources.

Being able to stay calm and ration food while avoiding excessive anxiety and stress is crucial to facing a crisis with clarity.

Even in difficult times, eating well and nourishing yourself properly helps maintain physical and mental health.

Planning ahead, being prepared, and adopting a calm and rational attitude are the best tools for effectively managing food resources during emergencies.

Chapter 8: The Importance of Drinking Water and Its Conservation

Water is the most vital resource in any emergency
situation.

While a person can survive for weeks without
food, survival without water is reduced to just a
few days.

In times of crisis, natural disasters, or service
interruptions, access to clean and drinkable
water can quickly become a problem. Water sources
may become contaminated, and the local water
system could stop functioning due to breakdowns,
blackouts, or contamination.

Being prepared to manage water is therefore
essential for ensuring survival and health.

One of the first steps to take is to have an
adequate reserve of drinking water for each
family member.

Guidelines suggest having at least 2-3 liters of
water per person per day, which covers drinking
needs and a small portion for cooking and
personal hygiene.

If you live in an area prone to natural disasters
or at risk of supply interruptions, it's
advisable to store enough water for at least two
weeks.

Reserves can be stored in sealed plastic bottles,
large containers, or specialized long-term
storage containers.

It's important to regularly check these supplies,
replacing water that may become stagnant or
contaminated.

In addition to quantity, it's important to ensure
that stored water remains clean and safe for
consumption.

Storing water in cool, dark environments helps
prevent the growth of bacteria or algae.

Containers should be tightly sealed and
sterilized before use. If you don't have a secure
storage system, water can be pre-treated with
purification tablets or unscented bleach.

Adding a few drops of bleach (approximately eight
drops per liter) can sterilize the water and make
it safe to drink.

However, it's important to use the correct type
of bleach and not to overdo the dosage, as this
could make the water toxic.

Beyond preparation and preventive storage, it's helpful to know alternative methods for obtaining drinkable water in emergencies.

Rainwater can be a valuable natural source but must be collected and treated properly.

Using clean buckets, jugs, or other containers to collect rainwater is an effective way to have an additional supply in case of need.

However, rainwater may also be contaminated by substances in the air or on collection surfaces, so it's essential to filter and treat it before use.

Using specific water filters or boiling it for at least ten minutes can eliminate most bacteria, viruses, and contaminants.

Another water source could be nearby water bodies such as rivers, lakes, or streams.

However, natural water is not always safe to drink without treatment.

Even if the water looks clean, it could contain pathogens, chemicals, or heavy metals.

In such cases, using portable filters, such as straw filters or gravity filtration systems, can ensure the water is safe for consumption.

There are advanced filters that can remove microscopic particles and dangerous contaminants, and these tools should be part of every family's emergency kit.

Again, boiling water is an ancient but effective practice that kills most pathogens and makes it safe to drink.

A crucial aspect of water management in emergency situations is conservation.

In times of scarcity, water must be used sparingly. This means avoiding waste and using water only for essential activities, such as drinking and cooking.

Minimizing use for personal hygiene and cleaning can make a big difference.

For example, washing hands with small amounts of water or using alcohol-based sanitizers instead of soap and water can preserve valuable resources.

Reusing water can also be a helpful strategy: water used for cooking, if not contaminated, can be reused for purposes such as cleaning surfaces or personal hygiene.

If you have a garden or vegetable patch, water may become essential for the survival of plants and food production.

In these cases, it's useful to adopt agricultural practices that minimize water consumption, such as drip irrigation or rainwater collection for irrigation.

Conserving water for plants can be an option, but it's essential to prioritize your own survival and not use more water than is strictly necessary.

Finally, it's crucial to be aware of potential contamination sources that could compromise water during an emergency.

Natural events like floods, earthquakes, or fires can pollute local water sources with mud, debris, or hazardous chemicals.

In crisis situations, it's vital to avoid using potentially contaminated water sources unless you have the means to treat them properly.

Listening to official communications about water safety is always the best choice. However, in the absence of information, it's better to treat all water as potentially contaminated, taking the necessary steps to purify it.

In conclusion, managing drinking water in an emergency context requires planning, awareness, and discipline.

Being prepared to collect, store, and treat water ensures not only survival but also the maintenance of health during a crisis.

Advance preparation and rational use of water resources are two key factors that can make the difference between a manageable situation and a catastrophic one.

Chapter 9: Evacuation Plans: How to Leave Home Safely

Being prepared to quickly leave your home in the event of an emergency is an essential aspect of overall preparedness.

An unexpected event like a fire, earthquake, flood, or conflict situation may require immediate evacuation, and having a well-defined plan can make the difference between leaving in an orderly fashion or being caught in chaos.

A well-designed evacuation plan should include not only a clear strategy for leaving the home but also adequate preparation for dealing with the days following the evacuation.

One of the main elements of an evacuation plan is knowledge of safe escape routes.

In any home, it's important to identify the main and alternative exits in advance and ensure they are always accessible.

If you live in a multi-story house, it may be useful to have a foldable ladder on hand to quickly descend from upper floors if necessary. This tool can be essential, especially if the internal stairs are impractical or if a main exit is blocked.

Another key aspect is having an "emergency bag" ready and easily accessible, commonly known as a "go bag." This bag should contain everything needed to survive for at least 72 hours, a period generally considered critical in the event of disasters.

The bag should include non-perishable food, water, a flashlight, spare batteries, a first aid kit, warm clothing, a copy of important documents (both paper and digital), cash, personal hygiene items, a portable radio, and communication devices.

It's also helpful to have a map of the area and to mark evacuation routes recommended by local authorities in case GPS systems fail.

Equally important is preparing a plan to reunite with family members in the event of sudden evacuation.

In a crisis situation, family members may be in different places, such as at school, work, or out of the house.

Having a predetermined meeting point, such as a friend's house or a safe area outside the city, helps minimize stress and uncertainty.

It's advisable to establish more than one meeting point in case the first is inaccessible and to ensure that all family members are aware of this plan and have the means to reach the destination independently if necessary.

Communication during an evacuation can be challenging. Phone lines may be overloaded or network services interrupted.

Devices like walkie-talkies or shortwave radios can ensure constant contact among family members, even in the absence of mobile signals.

It's also important to have an updated list of emergency phone numbers, including those of friends, relatives, and local authorities, printed in case digital contacts are lost.

If you have pets, their well-being must be incorporated into the evacuation plan.

Many people overlook this detail, but in an emergency situation, having a strategy to transport and care for animals is essential.

Ensure you have a separate bag with pet food, water, necessary medications, and a carrier to take them with you safely.

In addition to physical preparation, it's crucial to understand that emotions can be overwhelming during an evacuation. Fear, anxiety, and shock are natural reactions, but they can hinder the ability to make quick and rational decisions.

For this reason, it's useful to regularly practice the evacuation plan, so each family member knows what to do without having to think too much in a critical moment.

Conducting periodic drills allows you to identify any gaps in the plan and improve the effectiveness of the measures in place.

When planning an evacuation, consider the type of disaster you might face.

For example, in the case of a fire, it's essential to learn how to recognize danger signals, such as the smell of smoke or rising heat.

In these situations, it's crucial to remain calm, keep low to avoid inhaling toxic smoke, and exit immediately using the established escape routes.

In the event of flooding, it's important not to walk in deep water, as even a few inches can pose a drowning risk or be swept away by currents.

In the case of earthquakes, knowing how to protect yourself inside the home before evacuating—avoiding objects that could fall and staying away from windows and doors—is beneficial.

After leaving the home, it's essential to stay
informed about the situation's developments.

Local authorities and the media will be your
primary channels for receiving instructions on
when it's safe to return home or if you need to
relocate elsewhere.

Never return to the home until it has been
declared safe to do so. Even if the situation
seems to have stabilized, there may be invisible
risks, such as structural damage, gas leaks, or
exposed electrical wires.

In conclusion, being ready to evacuate your home
quickly requires detailed preparation and a
proactive mindset.

You can never predict when an emergency will
strike, but with a well-developed action plan,
you'll be able to leave home safely and manage
the uncertainty of the following period with
greater peace of mind.

Preparation not only offers you greater physical
protection but also a sense of control and
security, reducing the emotional and
psychological impact of a potentially traumatic
experience.

**Conclusion: Preparation is the Best Defense -
Chapter 10**

We live in an era where uncertainty is a constant.

Natural disasters, health emergencies, economic crises, and other unforeseen events can strike us without warning, putting our safety, our homes, and our well-being at risk.

However, as we have explored in this book, the key to facing any crisis is not fear, but preparation.

Being ready for anything means more than just stockpiling supplies or developing emergency plans.

It is a continuous commitment to protecting oneself and one's loved ones.

When we prepare, we are investing in our future and creating a safety net that will allow us to face challenges with confidence and resilience.

Emergencies cannot always be avoided, but how we respond to them can make the difference between suffering devastating losses or emerging stronger.

Preparation is not just a material matter; it is also mental and emotional.

Through organization, learning new skills, and careful planning, we put ourselves in a better position to control events rather than being overwhelmed by them.

We know where to go, what to bring, and how to protect ourselves and those we love.

We have learned that every detail, from creating an emergency kit to managing stress, plays a fundamental role in successfully navigating life's storms.

One of the central messages of this book is that prevention is always better than cure.

We cannot predict every threat, but we can prepare to face it. In a world where climate engineering and other global phenomena are making the future more unpredictable, adopting a proactive mindset becomes essential.

It is not about being paranoid or catastrophic; it is about recognizing that life can change in an instant and that having a plan means being ready to regain control, even when everything seems out of control.

Resilience is one of the greatest virtues we can develop. When we prepare our homes, our families, and ourselves for the worst, we equip ourselves with the tools to face difficulties with courage and determination.

We are building the capacity to rise again, no matter what happens. That is what makes the difference.

Being prepared does not mean passively waiting for a disaster to strike, but being ready to respond quickly, effectively, and with a clear mind.

The journey you have embarked on by reading this book is just the beginning. Now you have the knowledge and strategies to protect yourself from a wide range of scenarios.

What you do with this information is entirely up to you. Start today by implementing plans, building kits, practicing evacuations, and staying informed about potential risks. Every step you take brings you closer to safety.

Remember, preparation is an act of love towards yourself and those around you.

It is a demonstration of responsibility and awareness, a statement that, whatever happens, you will be ready.

Choose to leave nothing to chance and invest in what is most precious: your life, your home, and the people you love.

Thank you for reading this book and for understanding the importance of always being ready.

Now is the time to put into practice everything you have learned. Don't wait for an emergency to knock at your door.

Prepare your tomorrow today, and whatever happens, you will be ready to face it with courage and determination.

Good luck and always stay prepared.

Simone Azzurri

www.simoneazzurri.com
www.andiamosulpersonale.com

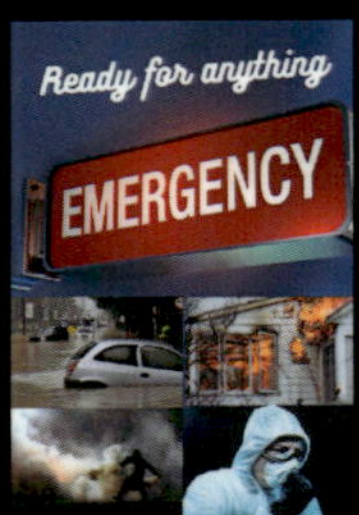

Why Prepare for Everything?
Preparing for everything is essential in a world where climate change and climate engineering are becoming ever-present realities.

With the artificial control of weather and the use of technologies to manipulate the climate, such as geoengineering and other advanced techniques, the natural balance of the environment is being altered, creating new and unpredictable conditions.

These interventions, often designed to mitigate global warming or manage extreme weather events, can nevertheless have unforeseen side effects.

For example, climate manipulation could cause storms, floods, droughts, or anomalous meteorological phenomena in areas where they were once rare or absent.

Having a well-structured home emergency plan becomes a necessity because adverse events are no longer entirely natural and, therefore, may strike with less warning.

Being prepared means not only facing events we are familiar with, such as blackouts or fires, but also adapting to new emergencies that may be triggered by artificial climate interventions.

ISBN 9798344148731